WHAT'S POSSIBLE IN RECOVERY?

Living in Fulfillment and Manifesting
the Treasure of Self-Discovery

Jay Jawitz

What's Possible in Recovery

Text by Jay Jawitz

2019 Team Fredom Coaching

Team Freedom Coaching

Visit our web site at www.teamfreedomcoaching.com

First edition 2019

ISBN: 978-1-7340163-0-7

CONTENTS

INTRODUCTION

I am a grateful person in recovery named Jay Jawitz. I stand as source for a transformed world. In August of 2001, I escaped a living hell called drug addiction. I immediately saw recovery as my opportunity of a lifetime. This was a perfect chance for me to completely transform my life. When we transform, we will discover the best version of ourselves. This is our authentic self. Our authentic self is the version of us that can create a life beyond our wildest dreams.

This book is an invitation to anyone who has suffered in addiction. I am giving you an invitation to leave the darkness of active addiction and step into the light of recovery. You can use my experiences to open you up to what is possible in recovery. The tools and strategy in this book will show you how to stop any addiction, change the way that you feel about yourself and the world around you.

If I can completely transform my life, then you can to. When you discover who you really are by living a new way of life, you will find that you are beautiful. I promise you that you matter, you are enough, and there is an incredible power inside of you that can only be shined on the rest of the world when you breakthrough the limiting beliefs that have been keeping you stuck. This world needs you to help battle addiction. In early recovery, I realized that I had been called to the winning side. Join myself and the many of others in this world that are living in recovery. If no one has told you that they love you, I will. I love you because I know that you have suffered. You no longer have to suffer.

GETTING CLEAN

In late July of 2001, I was about to go through the most grueling battle of my life. I was about to climb my way through the pits of hell with the hope that there was an escape route. I had been battling opioid addiction for nine years and was completely exhausted. I did not understand that the disease of addiction was a monster that was far greater then I am. I had got clean a couple of times before but could not stay clean for more than a couple of weeks. This was because I never understood my enemy. I thought my problem was the drug that I was taking, but later found out that the drugs were only a symptom of a lot larger
problem called addiction.

My world was crumbling down around me. I had been living a lie and carrying a secret. I had owed the firm that I worked for $80,000 for making a lot of bad decisions. I maxed out all my credit cards and owed creditors $50,000. I stole thousands of dollars from my parents. Most of my belongings were being given away to a pawn shop. I had accumulated a $1000 dollar a day habit, and I was out of ways and means to get more. The fear caused me to feel that the walls were caving in. Physically, I was sick all the time. I was six foot tall and weighed 125lbs. I nourished myself on candy and coffee. I could not look at myself in the mirror. I was spiritually, physically, and financially bankrupt. I had become the walking dead. My life had no meaning. I was in constant pain and suffering. There was only one thing I was doing right and did not even realize it. I was asking myself one incredibly empowering question. "Why am I here." Maybe there is a good reason for my existence. This question gave me just enough hope to exist another day. I believe this question was a tiny spark that was going to ignite an incredible blaze in the near future.

My little brother and a friend of mine were about to do an intervention. They asked me if I wanted to go fishing after work? Fishing was a passion of mine that had been slowly robbed by my addiction. I did not like the idea of going out on a boat. I had to put a needle in my arm about every four hours or I was going to be physically sick. I unwillingly agreed, because I had to conceal my addiction. When I arrived at the boat in the backyard of my parent's house, I was wondering why there were no fishing rods on the boat. My brother and Fernando got right to the point. They told me we were not going fishing. They both said that it is obvious that you have a serious problem and the game is up. They asked me "Do you want help." I surrendered but had no idea that I was surrendering to win.

My brother told my parents about my problem. I carried so much shame and guilt for the financial wreckage that I caused. Fear of their judgement was keeping me stuck, but I was about to be set free. It was difficult to explain to another person what it was like to have a physical addiction. My parents did not get me into a detox or treatment center. I told them that I can go through withdrawals at home even though it will be horrific.

On July 24, 2001 the battle began. It was my 29th birthday. A couple of hours before I was going to withdrawal, my parents had a family friend come over. This friend was Coach Greg Samuels. Greg was my tennis instructor and high school tennis coach. He was probably the only male role model that I ever completely trusted. Coach was a loving, kind, and wise person who I never witnessed judging others. Coach had my family get in a circle and he said a prayer. No one in my family ever talked of God, so the prayer was probably making my parents uncomfortable. All I could think about was the pain I was about to endure. Coach walked with me out to the dock in my parents backyard and wanted to have a talk with me. He proceeded to tell me that there are two main forces in the world. There is a force of good and there is a force of evil. Coach said addiction is a force of evil and I am going to have to discover some force of good if I am going to recover. The seed was planted. Coach left and I crawled into bed with a state of total certainty that I would be experiencing the worst pain of my life. I also knew that there was no turning back. The house was locked down and my parents were committed to looking over me as long as it took. I had my dog Brandy at my side. She was my angel. Dope sickness from 2400mg of oxycontin daily is like food poisoning X 20 with every bone in your body aching. I will spare you the graphic details.

After three days of horrific illness, I felt good enough to turn on the television. I hit the remote and the first thing that appeared was the movie Shawshank Redemption. This was my favorite movie of all time. I started to cry because I could not deny that some force of good was starting to work in my life. I did not believe that this was a coincidence. Toward the end of the movie "Red" played by Morgan Freeman said "Get busy living or get busy dying." When I heard this, I was overwhelmed with emotion and cried like never before. It felt like I was breaking down but I know today that I was starting to break free. It had occurred to me that I had been killing myself on the installment plan. Next, Morgan Freeman said that he "was about to embark on a new journey that only a free man can feel." At that moment, I made a decision to embark on a new journey of my own.

THE SOLUTION

I am forever grateful to my mother for finding me an ongoing solution to the disease of addiction. My mother was calling drug rehabilitation centers and by accident called the helpline number to a 12step fellowship. My parents were called back immediately and were met with a compassionate ear. My parents were directed to send me to my first 12step meeting. I was open to doing anything to not go back to the hell that I just escaped. I know today that I was given the best gift a recovering addict can receive. I was given the Gift of Desperation(GOD.)

I was given directions to a meeting on a Tuesday night at 8:00 PM. I was a little apprehensive and fearful, but I was open. I carried a lot of shame and guilt for the mess that I created. The last thing I was going to need was judgement or ridicule. I arrived to the parking lot at about five minutes before the meeting started. A few seconds after I stepped out of the car, I was greeted by a guy named Matt. He asked me "have you ever been to a meeting before." I said no, and he embraced me with a hug. He proceeded to tell me that I was going to be the most important person at the meeting. I did not understand exactly what he meant, but it felt good. I didn't know that I mattered. The unconditional love I experienced in that moment opened me up for what was coming next. I walked into a room of about

80 people. It seemed that there were various types of people from different walks of life. There was a collective energy in the room that gave me a positive vibe. Everyone seemed to be happy and getting along with one another. People were greeting one another with hugs and I was not excluded. I felt safe. The meeting started with some readings. As I listened, so many things started to make sense as if pieces of a puzzle were coming together. As the speaker shared his experience, I saw many similarities within myself. I know today that it is critical to focus on similarities with others and not our differences. I was starting to experience hope and unconditional love for the first time in my life. I believed that I never had to use substances ever again and I could change. If people just like me were staying clean, than I could to. I know today Hope and Love are the only spiritual principles you can give to another. Each moment in that meeting seemed to be better than the next.

By the end of that meeting, I felt like I arrived. It got even better when the meeting was over. Several people came over and introduced themselves to me. Everyone was giving me hugs and introducing me to more people. Some people asked me questions and just listened to me. Some people shared their experience, strength, and hope for a couple minutes. Nobody judged me or ridiculed me. Everyone made me feel welcome. I immediately came to understand that going to 12 step meetings was an environment where I could stop using and heal.

I came to the understanding that becoming a member of a 12 step program and following that program was an incredible opportunity for me to experience freedom from active addiction. It was also an incredible opportunity to change my life. I was given several suggestions at that first meeting. When I heard the suggestions, I realized that staying clean was going to require a lot of work and serious commitment. For the first time in my life I was willing to do whatever it took. I was willing to do everything suggested because I did not want to go back to the hell that I came from. I also knew in a state of certainty that if I did the work and took the suggestions I was going to get results. I was shown by the experience of others that I could completely transform my life. I was shown that if I change, I will feel better about who I am. The experience of others showed me that by changing and growing, I will just start to feel better. I was going to be given tools to become the master of my own influence. With this being said, the work that is required in recovery will not seem like work because of the incredible rewards that come along with it. The other alternative is to live in the hell called active addiction. The work that is required to live in active addiction is incredibly hard and painful. This awful work gives you a tiny bit of instant gratification with a side order pain, misery, and suffering. For me, the choice was a no-brainer. I became committed to doing whatever it took to get the results. I always tried to apply the quote that helped get me clean.

"Get busy living or get busy dying"

Steven Speilberg

Once we are clean, we are given the power of choice. For me it was very effective to have clear distinctions. I tried to see most things in recovery as black and white. This kept me from getting confused in the grey area and helped me to make proper decisions. I chose to get busy living, so I became committed to my recovery. I was told that recovery is a precious gift and always must come first in my life. I must not let anything get in the way of my recovery. Recovery was defined to me as abstinence plus change. I started to change right away because I was open to shifting my beliefs. As I listened to literature and others in the meetings, I started to take on beliefs that were setting me up to win. Here are some beliefs that I took on, which set me up to win.

1. I never have to use again.
2. I can change.
3. I am deserving of the gifts of recovery.
4. By using, my life will always get worst and never better.
5. Addiction lives in my mind.
6. Playing the role of the victim will keep me stuck.
7. It's the first one that kills me.
8. I cannot recover alone.
9. Everything happens for a reason.
10. Life is happening for me.
11. I am not my past.
12. I have something to give others.
13. I must grow and change.
14. A grateful person in recovery will never use.
15. I must practice Honesty like my life depends on it.

Taking on new beliefs helped me to deflate the ego that had

been killing me. This demolition of my ego kept me open to suggestions and taking on a new way of life.

Here are the basic suggestions that were given to me.

1. Attend 90 meetings in 90 days and then attend meetings regularly
2. Get a sponsor who is someone with experience to guide you through the program.
3. Work the steps
4. Build a support group of people in recovery
5. Change old people, places and things.

I started to go to meetings every day. I would see some of the same people over and over again, even though I was going to meetings all over town. I was constantly meeting new people, learning new things, and hearing new amazing stories. Life in recovery was becoming exciting. After a couple of weeks I got myself a sponsor. I started calling him every day and started becoming accountable. He gave me something to read on acceptance. That little reading changed my life. I never had practiced acceptance in my life before recovery. I started to experience peace and serenity because I realized that I could not control situations. I also realized that the world did not revolve around me. Understanding and practicing acceptance helped open me up to believing in God.

After my lesson in acceptance, I was given an assignment to write out a gratitude list. I started to put the list together. The first few things were I am alive, I have a roof over my head, and I am not in prison. The fourth thing that came up created a major breakthrough. It had occurred to me that I lost the obsession and compulsion to use drugs. This was monumental because I knew that everything I was learning was working. As I went over the gratitude list with my sponsor he pointed out that a grateful addict will never use. This helped me shift from a person who was always a victim to a person who became grateful for everything. I learned to become grateful for the things that showed up that some people would call bad. These were things that gave me the opportunity to grow and practice the tools that I was using. I became grateful for everything because I was shown that I have the power to decide what things mean. I would choose empowerment because I was committed to my growth.

After my lesson in acceptance and gratitude I started to learn about honesty. For the most part, I lied to myself and those around me before I got clean. I started to realize that there was incredible freedom when I became honest. The weight of the world was off my shoulders. Covering up lies all the time was exhausting. By practicing honesty, I was given the freedom to be me. I sure as hell was not perfect, but I was constantly getting better. Making a commitment to practice honesty in all my affairs allowed me to feel better about myself. I stopped lying, cheating and stealing. Practicing honesty allowed me to take personal responsibility. Self-Honesty gave me the ability to always change, shift and learn from my past experiences. Honesty helped pave the way for a complete transformation. The incredible success I was having in my early recovery was due to surrendering completely. All I did was model an effective strategy.

MODELING EFFECTIVE STRATEGY

I f you want to achieve any goal in life there is a simple success formula.

1. Know what you want
2. Know why you want it
3. Take a plan of action or strategy
4. Know if your strategy is working

Thomas Edison tried 10,000 times before he invented the electrical lightbulb. He changed his strategy again and again until he found success.

How does this apply to recovery? Here is your wake up call! The disease of addiction is deadly. You do not have as many tries as Thomas Edison available to you. If you have not succeeded in the past, there are some good reasons why. You must surrender completely to an effective strategy if you are to recover and stay clean. If you are not committed to a strategy, your diseased mind will make plans for you and you will pick up again. If you want to get out of pain and start to experience the infinite possibilities recovery has to offer you, model an effective strategy. If you are going to model an effective strategy, choose one that has worked for a number of people. Find at least 10 people that have followed a strategy, and have been in recovery for at least a few years. Ask them the details of their strategy. After asking 10 people, you will start to notice consistent patterns and then you can make an informed decision. It is important not to let the ego or diseased mind make decisions for us.

I cannot tell you what strategy to choose. I will only share my experience. Before I got clean, I received all my information from misinformed people or people that did not have my best interests in mind. Examples of these people were people I used with, or pain management clinics that profited by becoming my new drug dealer. I tried to get clean on my own over and over again, but I always would pick up again. I would feel worst about myself each time. I would start to take on the belief that I was a failure or hopeless. I was lying to myself every day. When I went to my first 12 step meeting I was given the hope that I needed and I was shown a strategy on how to stay clean and recover. I was told that the strategy has a 100% success rate, if I follow the strategy in it's entirety. This is the strategy that was shown to me that I still use today.

1. I had to eliminate being in contact with drugs or alcohol, or people that were using.
2. Attend 12 step meetings regularly. It was suggested to attend 90 meetings in 90 days in the beginning.

15

3. Get a sponsor(someone who guides you through a 12- step program.)

4. Start working the 12 steps with your sponsor.

5. Form a support group of others in recovery and call those people every day.

6. Get a home group. A home group is one of your meetings that you always attend so you can be accountable.

As I started going to various meetings every day, I saw some very consistent patterns. The strategy that was suggested was the same at every meeting I went to. I have been a person in recovery since August of 2001, and have attended meetings on every corner of the United States. I have met people in recovery from all over the world. The strategy that they use is the same. This strategy has been working for thousands and thousands of people in recovery from all over the world for way over half of a century.

Some people fail in recovery because they do not follow an effective strategy in it's entirety. We will use my wife as an example. I met my wife when I had eight years clean. She had nine years clean. I have had the pleasure of listening to my wife share her experience, strength and hope in meetings and institutions many times. Her experience is completely different then mine. The only thing that is the same is the strategy that we have been following for years. My wife was shown the same strategy that she uses in recovery today over and over again before she stayed clean. She claimed that she would use salad bar recovery. This meant that she picked and chose parts of the strategy the way you would pick food on a salad bar. She would use parts of the strategy that seemed very convenient but not surrender to it's entirety. She made an assumption that if she took half of the suggestions she would feel 50% better. Recovery never works this way, and it certainly didn't work for her. This would be the same as following the recipe for a great cake and leaving out the sugar and flour. The result will not be the one you are looking for.

Remember; this is your life we are talking about. Choose an effective strategy and follow it in it's entirety. This way you will start to discover the infinite possibilities recovery has to offer. As you experience the incredible results you will become source for others. You will become a shining example that others can model. How cool is that? You will be making the world a better place by taking care of yourself and empowering others.

STOPPING ANY ADDICTION

How do we stop any addiction? Addiction is a powerful monster. Stopping an addiction can be like getting a 1000lb gorilla off your back. Getting the gorilla off your back appears difficult. With the help of guidance from others, and stepping into your personal power you can be free. You cannot begin to imagine just how powerful you are. The only way to tap into your power is to become the master of your own influence.

If you want freedom from any addiction you must first take 100% responsibility. Addiction lives in your brain. Look at your brain as a computer with faulty wiring . Nobody can re-wire your brain but you. You can allow others to guide you but you have to do the work.

When I had been in recovery for about 3 weeks, I had lost the obsession and compulsion to use drugs or alcohol. I was going to meetings every day and really paying attention. I was holding on to every word like my life depended on it. I was given an assignment by my sponsor to write out a gratitude list. I had to write 25 things that I was grateful for. When I was thinking about the next thing to put on the list, I realized that I did not feel like getting high today. I could not remember when was the last time I thought about getting high. It must have been a few days back. I became overwhelmed with gratitude because I realized that the obsession and compulsion to use had been lifted. This seemed like a miracle because I could not seem to break that obsession and compulsion for nine years.

Did the obsession and compulsion really just lift? It has never came back, but that is because I was applying a tool that was being shown to me. I had taken a suggestion that I heard. Because I had been going to meetings every day, I was hearing people share with a burning desire that they wanted to get high.

There was an old timer that would sit in the back of one of my meetings named Steve M. He said if you feel like using, play the tape all the way through. What he meant was to start associating the inevitable consequences with the thought of using. This was in September of 2001, so people still owned tape players. Any particular addiction is nothing more than a pattern in the brain. If we are to stop an addiction, that pattern must be interrupted. In early recovery almost anything can cause a using thought. They are happening all the time. It is up to us to take consistent action when thoughts come up. If I had a using thought, I would immediately visualize a tape player. I would picture all the buttons in a row. There was a play, pause, stop, record, fast forward and rewind button. I would picture the tip of my index finger hitting the fast forward button. I would even imagine the sound that the film in the tape would make when fast forwarding. I would now start to associate using with massive amounts of immediate pain, misery and suffering. For me I thought about dope sickness, suffering, isolation, disconnection, desperation, financial burden, harming others, possible incarceration, and death. I would also think about the painful things that did not happen yet such as prison or death. This would disrupt the pattern in my brain. Before I used this tool, my brain would associate using with pleasure. Once we use this leverage on ourselves by interrupting the pattern, our brain starts to associate the thought of using with pain. Once we interrupt the pattern, we must create an alternative pattern. The pattern that I came up with is; if I don't use I get to be in recovery. When I get to be in recovery, I open myself up to infinite possibilities. I get to experience happiness, joy, freedom, excitement, peace, healing, love, forgiveness, purpose, passion, abundance and so much more. Now my brain would associate not using with pleasure. This whole process is called using leverage through neuro-associative conditioning. We use this tool so our brain makes a new neuro-association. Our brain is making new neuro-associations all the time. To keep it simple, you can call the technique fast-forwarding the tape.

A couple of years ago I was challenged with an ice cream addiction. I loved ice cream and was only eating about a cup once a week and it was not a problem. One night I ate a little more because my wife allowed me to taste her new flavor. I went to the gym early the next morning to train my legs and got a pump like never before. I was talking about my workout with a sports medicine coach and told him about my incredible pump. He asked me what changed and he started reviewing my nutrition. He said that there is a chance that the pump in my legs came from eating all the sugar the night before. That sounded good to me, so I justified eating ice cream every day. A few months later ice cream was making my life unmanageable. I was going out to the store at night to get more. I was eating my step son's ice cream. I was getting acid reflux every time I ate ice cream. I still had a beautiful six pack but it was hiding under a 10lb gut. I have learned that when the pain gets great enough, I will do something about it. I wanted to stop so I started to apply leverage. I started to fast forward the tape. I would associate ice cream with acid reflux, possible diabetes, doctor bills, and being out of shape. I pictured myself 10 years down the road if I was eating ice cream every day. It was not a pretty sight. I interrupted the pattern, and created a new neuro association. I started to associate not eating ice cream with health, feeling good, being fit, and looking good. I have never had ice cream again. If you like ice cream, keep enjoying it. If you want to stop, apply leverage by fast forwarding the tape. I recently discovered that I can become addicted to looking at my phone. This does not become a major problem until the wheels of my vehicle are moving. I survived an accident at the age 7, when I was on a bus that dropped 80ft of the side of a mountain. It would be tragic to allow an addiction to kill me in a car accident that could have been prevented. I started to apply leverage with this addiction. If I want to look at my phone while the car is moving, I start to think about what it would be like to wake up in a coma and find out that I am responsible for murder. I have now set a boundary that if I am in my car and driving, I can only look down at the phone when the wheels are not moving. If you want to stop anything, take responsibility and fast forward the tape.

ALL-STAR TEAM

One of the key elements to success in any area of life is having a great team. In recovery, having a team is critical. You are probably not going to stay clean very long without the help of others. Because the diseased mind speaks to you in your own voice, you want to avoid being trapped in your head with nothing but your own thoughts. Your best thinking is what got you into trouble in the first place. Once we surrender and deflate our ego, we can allow others to help us and start to create our all-star team. If you are going to battle the monster called addiction, why not create a powerful army. Once you allow others in, you start to become higher powered.

When I went to my first 12-step meeting, the chairperson asked if there were any people that were new. I put my hand up because I was there to get help. After the meeting I was approached with kindness. People gave me hugs and made me feel welcome. They shared their experience for a couple of minutes but most of all they listened. I grew up in a household where no one ever listened and what I had to say did not matter. My feelings were never validated and I became closed off to really becoming connected with others because I was afraid to be myself. For the first time ever in my life, people listened without judgement. I found people that understood my terrible circumstances. I felt that I can be vulnerable for the first time in my life, and that I was not alone.

Several people gave me their phone numbers and showed me how to access meetings in my local area. I started calling a few people every day, and I would talk for a couple of minutes and make a plan to meet them at a meeting. I started to go out to dinner or coffee with some of the people after meetings. Becoming accountable and receiving hope from others in recovery was helping me to not think about getting high.

In 12 step recovery it is critical to have a sponsor. After a couple of weeks, I met my first sponsor. A sponsor is another person in recovery who guides you through a 12 step program. I asked him to sponsor me because I related to his childhood when he shared his story. He also had a passion for recovery. He would say "you will never believe in your wildest dreams what will happen to you if you go to meetings regularly and work the steps." He filled me up with hope and opened me up to infinite possibility. Having someone believe in me when I never believed in myself, shifted everything. This helped me to become motivated and deeply committed to what was suggested by others.

I have had three sponsors in 17 years of recovery. My first sponsor opened me up to infinite possibility. My second sponsor was not a man of many words. He kept things completely simple. All my sponsors were someone that I could trust and were always there for me. They all taught me different things.

My current sponsor and I, have had a relationship for thirteen years. He is the best listener I have ever known. I have never felt judged by him. He has never told me what to do and he never pointed a finger at me. He has always been a stand for my greatness and has taught me how my limited beliefs have kept me stuck. He always returns my calls and is the person who is standing right there when I wake up from a five hour operation. He is the man that knows everything about me. When we first started together he said that your diseased mind will try to pitch you lies and my job is to help you to not buy into those lies.

I have learned in life that water will always seek it's own level. You will be a direct result of the team you surround yourself with. I choose to create my team with people that have high standards for their self and will always empower me to be my best. If you are going to create your recovery team, you must choose wisely. You will learn who is best for your recovery. When you see people cosigning behavior that is not in line with honesty and integrity beware. Remember; this is your transformed life we are talking about. Make sure you choose a team that always comes from love by looking out for your best interests.

As you progress in your recovery, so will your experiences. I promise you that life will always show up. Sometimes there might not be someone on your immediate team that will have all the answers. You might be experiencing a situation that is not familiar with someone on your team. This is where you get the chance to expand your team, and make new connections.

KNOWING YOUR ENEMY

How can you win a battle if you do not even know your enemy? When I arrived at my first 12 step meeting, I thought my problem was Oxycontin or any other opiod. I thought that if I can get the drugs out of my body and no longer have a physical habit, I would be fine. I had no problem admitting that I was an addict. I had an obsessive and compulsive nature with everything from the time I was seven years old. Back then this showed up with girls, candy, baseball cards, fishing, video games and sports. I can't tell you how many times my brain would say one more to all of these things. If my brain said one more, I would just keep going. My brain was lying to me. One more seemed to always be the story of my life. I bought into that lie until I started to step into my power in recovery. I didn't know I was an addict until my drug use. After two years of using drugs I would start to cross the line. I would make a decision that my consequences would only go so far. If I crossed the line that I set, I would just set a new line. I didn't know that I suffered from a progressive and mental illness called addiction.

At my first meeting, I learned that my problem was not the substance, but the problem was with my thinking. The substance is only the symptom of a lot larger problem. It was good news to find out that my only enemy was in my head.

When we get honest and take personal responsibility we can see the disease for what it is and accept it. I learned that there does not have to be shame in accepting the disease. The crazy thing is that once we admit defeat we start to empower ourselves and set are self up to win. I am proud to say that I am a person in recovery. You can look at the disease as a little monster that lives in your head and attaches to the ego. I call the disease a little monster because it can be kept in it's cage when we use the tools that recovery teaches us. When we are using, the monster becomes big and will destroy everything. The disease is tricky, sneaky, insidious, cunning and feeds off our limiting beliefs. The disease is always negative and never gives us a good suggestion. The disease wants us to keep secrets, tell lies, and where a mask. The disease does not want you to accept yourself. The disease will try to get you to second guess yourself when you make good decisions. The disease will try to distract you from doing the next right thing and your recovery. The disease does not want you to experience freedom, peace, happiness, joy and gratitude. The disease is never going away. It will be there to the day you die. Even if you stay clean for the rest of your life, the disease will show up in some other form if you are not fulfilled.

Here is the great news. When we start to recover we become conscious and start to wake up. We start to realize what is a diseased thought and we can teach ourselves to laugh at it or let it pass. I like to laugh at it, and say good try, or F_ _ _ you. I give you permission to get pissed off at your disease. Once we are aware of our disease, we have the power of choice. We can watch the disease attempt to sabotage our recovery and become grateful when we do not listen to it. It is important for us to keep acknowledging ourselves for doing the next right thing and not listening to the disease. Meditation can be a great tool to quiet it down.

We are not responsible for having the disease but we must be responsible for becoming the masters of our own influence. We must be responsible for our recovery. Once we do this we begin to transform and open ourselves up to infinite possibility.

SPIRITUALLY AWAKENED

When I had about 3 months clean, I felt like I was on fire. Everything seemed to be falling in place. I can tell you that things were not working out exactly the way that I planned, but that is because I was allowing a higher power to start working in my life. Life was always showing up and it was always great opportunity for me to grow and practice the principles I was learning. I was experiencing happiness, freedom and excitement every day. Things were going so great and I felt unworthy. There was a part of me that knew all the harm that I caused in my past and felt like I should be punished for my past. The reality was that I already had punished myself. I was worthy of the gifts of recovery and so are you. Even though I did not yet believe in God. I believed that others believed, and their relationship with God was working for them. They all said that the God of their understanding was always loving and never punishing. I was grateful that I was allowed to come to believe instead of having to take on someone else's belief. The only stipulation was that the power was loving. The last thing that I needed was someone else's dogma. That would of blocked me from my own process. Just when you think everything is going great, you discover that there is another level.

When I had 102 days clean, my sponsor brought me to a meeting in a jail as a form of doing service. I was apprehensive, but I trusted the man that was helping me stay clean and discover a new way of life. When we arrived to the front of the jail, he proceeded to tell me that tonight was going to be a night that I remember for the rest of my life. He said that I will be chairing the meeting and telling my story on cell block A2 and he was going to cover the meeting on cell block A1. I heard a voice in my head say "Houston we have a problem."

My response to my sponsor was "that is not going to happen." He asked "why." I said that I do not speak in front of a group of people. He asked "why." I happened to have a great story and I had some pride because I was telling the truth. Honesty was a still new concept for me. He said "lets hear it." When I was in college I had a presentation to give in front of a classroom of about 40 people. This was my last class to graduate. I had already been away at college for seven years to get a four year degree. About a minute into my presentation, I froze up. I looked like a deer with headlights on it's face. My heart was beating very fast. Sweat was starting to drip down my arm pits. I started to feel self-conscious and it felt like I was being judged. I did not know what to do, so I ran out of the classroom and never came back. I never contacted the teacher and avoided the people in that class the rest of the semester. It was easier for me to fail the class and go back to college another semester, than face my embarrassment.

My sponsor replied "that is a great story but you are in recovery now." He said that you are starting to practice honesty, acceptance, surrender, gratitude, and hope but now you get to practice faith and courage. There was a part of me that wanted to run but I had nowhere to go. He said that I have nothing to lose because I will never see any of the guys in the jail ever again.

I unwillingly agreed to share my story. I got up in front of 50 guys in blue jump suits and said that I am an addict in recovery named Jay. I don't want to be here because I don't like speaking in front of people. I said bear with me and maybe you will get something out of what I have to share. I was starting to share my experience, strength and hope. About five minutes into my message I realized that I was talking in front of people and they actually seemed very interested in what I had to say.

About 20 minutes later my sponsor came over and was trying to get me to wrap it up. The guy who could not speak in front of people, could not shut up. I had so much to say about finding a new way to live in recovery. When I opened the meeting up for sharing, lots of hands went up. People shared that my message had given them hope. The audience was inspired to check out meetings. I realized that if I could speak in front of people and give them hope, then there must be a God. This was my burning bush miracle. I went from wondering if there was a God to knowing that there was a God. I also knew that this God had an incredible plan and purpose for my life. I realized that my purpose is to carry the message to the addict who is still suffering. It became very clear that the question I was asking myself while I was living in hell was answered. Before I got clean, I wondered why I existed. Now I knew my purpose. It had occurred to me that I had to go through hell to get to heaven. I believe that heaven is a state of mind. All because I practiced some faith and courage; I discovered the God of my understanding, my voice, and my purpose all in one evening. My sponsor was not kidding when he said that it was going to be a night that I would remember for the rest of my life. That experience showed me that nothing great ever happens in your comfort zone.

The next morning, the world looked like a completely different place. I felt like I belonged to the rest of the world and knew that I had something to give. Discovering my purpose gave me incredible drive and passion. All of the sudden, nothing else mattered but living my purpose. I started living my life like I was source for others to recover. I would live my life as if others were always watching me. I started to take actions as if my life and the lives of others depended on it. The consequences of my addiction and my past baggage stopped bothering me because I knew I was going to have the opportunity to make amends. I really was starting to arrive in the present moment. I had the faith that if I live my purpose, God was going to take care of the rest.

My life became very simplified. All I had to do was not use, continuously grow and be of service to others. I started to give my painful past new meaning. I realized that I suffered in the past so I can awaken spiritually and start to become conscious. I was starting to believe that life would happen for me and not to me. I became aware that life is always showing up. If life was not always showing up than I would not have the incredible opportunity to learn, grow and change. I started to come to the understanding that change does not take a long time. Change happens the moment you make a committed decision to change. Growth would happen when I would take the tools and principles that I was learning and apply them in my life. As I started to apply spiritual principles in my life, I started to discover my authentic self.

I started to become a vacuum for growth and self-discovery. Every time I would grow, have a breakthrough, or have a new awareness I would feel better. My brain started to associate growth and change with feeling good. If that is the case, then why not take growth and change to another level and feel great. I didn't stop there. I kept creating momentum with my growth and change until I started to experience bliss.

Right after my spiritual awakening in jail, I started to throw my hands up in meetings and share. I would share my experiences with the intent of carrying a message to others through my own transformation. Some old timers would say that new comers should shut up and listen.I call bull___on that.I discovered my voice and you better believe that I was going to use it. Many people new to recovery suffer from low self-esteem and never had a voice in their own life. The last thing anyone needs to hear is shut up and you have nothing to say. Don't get me wrong, I agree that most do not want to be preached to. In a 12 step environment, we carry a message to one another through are own experience. If you have experience, share it with others. It is critical that we do more listening, but starting to share your experiences allows you to become a contribution.

When we enter the flow of creating new experiences and sharing them with others, we start to experience fulfillment. Fulfillment for any human being only happens when we are growing and being a contribution. The more I would share my experience with the intent of passing on hope, the more I would want to learn and grow. This flow would propel me into momentum. Sharing my experiences with others would allow me to connect to others at a higher level. This would allow me to experience significance and increase my self-worth. It becomes easy to increase your self- worth when you become committed to doing the next right thing and helping others. This transformation in recovery brought me from hating myself to loving myself within four months. I spent my whole life before recovery wanting to be someone other than myself. For the first time in my life I did not want to be anyone but me. I was grateful for this incredible gift.

When we allow ourselves to become spiritually awakened in recovery, we transform. Our metamorphosis can be compared to a caterpillar becoming a butterfly. We transform into a semi-ugly worm into a beautiful butterfly. Before the caterpillar becomes beautiful it has to spend time in the chrysalis. Our time spent in the darkness of our chrysalis can seem painful. Our struggle to get out of the dark builds our strength. This strength is necessary if we are going to step into our power and learn to fly. Once we grow our wings and discover our beauty, we are ready to fly around others to show them what is possible. We will never see our own beauty if we do not leave the dark of our chrysalis and enter the light. We will find that the gift is in the giving.

SOUL SEARCHING

Are you willing to let go of who you have become to be who you are? Who are you? I can promise you that you are not your past. If you do not know exactly who you are, start to ask yourself empowering questions such as why are you here, what is your purpose, and what major contribution do you have to give to this world.

Many people in early recovery are not open to looking deep into their past because of fear of what they might find. They either do not want to experience emotions from trauma or a painful past. This could set you up for a relapse. Remember, you are not your past. When you discover your authentic self, you will find that you matter, you are enough, you are loveable, and there is incredible power inside of you that can only be shined on the rest of the world when you breakthrough the limiting beliefs that keep you stuck. Stop running from yourself. You are beautiful.

If you are looking for total freedom, you must muster up some courage and dig into your whole life history. You want to go far back as you can remember. We dig all the way into our past for a few reasons. We get to discover who we are and who we are not. We get to look at all the facts of our past with a new interpretation. We get to look at the exact nature of our wrongs and take responsibility. We get to take a look at labels that were put on ourselves by others. We get to discover our limiting beliefs that keep us stuck and keep us from living our dream life. We get to discover who we need to make amends to down the road. We get to discover people that we need to forgive if we are to be free. In the future, we will get to see how our past experiences can be beneficial to others freedom. It is going to take a lot of work but the reward of total freedom is an incredible payoff. You cannot put a price on total freedom. Once you are completely free from your past, you will open yourself up to living your dream life.

My earliest memory as a child was my parents taking me to Disney World. I was not even three years old. My mother thought it would be a great idea to put me on a roller coaster in the dark called space mountain. My mother placed me on my father's lap. My father was arguing with my mother that it was a bad idea. As my father started to hold me tightly, I felt his fear. The ride went up, down, and all around. Within a couple of minutes I was traumatized. I was having a temper tantrum and started to experience anger, fear, and distrust for the first time. I was scared of every ride the rest of the day. Even though the rest of the rides were slow, happy, and joyful I was seeing nothing but my past experience. My parents could not console me because of my wall of distrust. After my first Day at Disney World, I started to create a belief that I always have to worry and live in fear.

When I was five years old my parents took me to a place in

North Miami where there were pony rides. My little brother and I were placed on separate ponies. My pony decided to sneak out of the corral and run down the street. They sent a man on a horse after the runaway pony. The pony was walked to the stable with me on the back of it. I was having a temper tantrum and screaming at my mother. This incident had nothing to do with my mother but my perception at the time was different. I started to take on a belief that bad things were always going to happen and my mother planned it that way. I spent my whole life before recovery placing blame on my parents. I started to take on the role of victim.

My parents were not completely terrible. My perception was skewed a lot of the time. I am grateful that my parents were always supportive of my interests. My father spent a lot of time with me showing me love and supporting my interests. I really loved animals as a kid. When I was five, my parents took me to a pond to feed the ducks. They left me alone with a loaf of bread. I started to make friends with a duck and soon I had a couple of new friends. A little later I had a few more friends. The next thing you know there were ducks everywhere. My new friends lost their manners and started to get greedy. They were getting out of control with the quacking and pecking. They backed me into the pond where I was up to my waist in water. I surrendered the bread and started to scream for help. My parents finally got out of the car and did nothing but laugh at me. I felt humiliated. I started to take on a belief that I was the source of my parents entertainment and always had to worry about being judged.When I was seven years old my parents sent me to sleepaway camp in North Carolina for eight weeks. I was from South Florida and was never away from home before. After two weeks of camp, the children my age were going to be taken on a 3 day campout in the Pisgah National Forrest. I was very excited until the bus started driving up a mountain cliffhanger road. All the kids on the bus were having a great time doing what seven year old children do on a bus. I was the only one who was not having a great time. I looked out the window of the bus, and all I saw was a several hundred foot drop. My gut was telling me that something was wrong. I was filled with fear and did nothing but worry until the bus reached the top of the mountain where there was a large beautiful clearing. On the back side of the clearing there was a waterfall where you could slide down the rocks. Camping out was a lot of fun. The next day they were going to take 20 kids to a place called Big Sliding Rock. I was the last kid to get on the bus. The bus started to go down the mountain cliffhanger road. We started driving for about a minute, and the bus started to swerve as we went around a hairpin turn. The bus dropped off the side of the road and dropped about eighty feet. The bus got caught alongside a giant tree. If it was not for that tree we would of dropped another several hundred feet to the bottom of the gorge. As the bus rolled over in the air there was light piercing through the trees. I thought I was about to die and all I could think about was that I was right. I knew there was something wrong with the whole situation from the moment we started going up that road on the first day of the campout. My ego was justified in creating the belief that fear and worry were always necessary for my survival.

When the bus landed things got crazy but I was already in

survival mode. I was wedged under a bench seat and struggled to pry myself loose. The counselors were both in a coma. There were kids screaming for their mothers. There was blood everywhere but my self preservation made me numb to my surroundings. I was unharmed physically. I only had a few scratches. Myself and two other boys managed to climb up to the road to get help. I remember I was climbing behind a boy named Aaron whose red converse high top came off his foot as he was climbing. I said to him "Hey, what about your shoe." He didn't even care and just kept climbing. A jeep showed up from the forest service who brought us down the mountain. The next thing you know there were helicopters and ambulances. Nobody had died but the injuries were very serious. I found out 35 years later that the road was turned into a mountain bike trail. Several vehicles had gone over at the same spot. Some people did not make it.

A vehicle from the state forest service brought some of us to the closest hospital. I remember how scared I was to drive in a car after that experience. At the hospital I got to have ice cream which can make any kid better for a few minutes. I also got to call my parents. I asked my mother "when are you coming to pick me up and bring me home from summer camp?" Her reply was "we are not picking you up because you will be at summer camp for another six weeks." My parents acted like nothing had happened to me. They discounted the fact that I was in a traumatizing accident. I started to take on a belief that my feelings did not matter.

After a few hours in the hospital I was taken back to summer camp. I was on medical watch in the camp infirmary for a couple days. I was there all by myself. The only person who came to visit me was a pretty fifteen year old girl named Evie. She called me her camp boyfriend. She payed attention to me and called me cute. She would give me a kiss on the cheek. I believe she gave me everything that was missing in my relationship with my mother. Evie became my first addiction. I no longer wanted to go back home. I wanted to stay in summer camp as long as possible. My parents came up on visiting day, and all I could think about was being away from Evie for the day. This was the beginning of my addiction to the opposite sex. I started to take on a limiting belief that I am not alright without a girlfriend.

When I was nine years old I had a crush on a girl named Jodi. She was the queen of fourth grade. One weekend I was at my grandparents house. My grandparents did not understand why I was locked in a bedroom all weekend on the phone. I was on the phone with Jodi and asked her to go steady. On Sunday night she said yes. I must have been the happiest boy in the world that night. I was so looking forward to holding her hand the next day in school. When I arrived at school the next day, Jodi had her arm around someone else. I was crushed and was a mess the next few days. I looked at the boy she had her arm around, and I started to take on the belief that I am not good enough.

Comparing myself with others and feeling less than was a common theme for me until I came into recovery. This showed up in my life all the time. It didn't help that I was always compared to my brother by my parents. I was also compared to other kids in sports by my father. My father would be extremely supportive when I did well in sports. If I made a simple mistake he would lose his temper. I remember when I was seven years old, I ran in on a fly ball in T-ball. When I missed the ball, I got a lecture the whole way home from the game. I always took everything personally from my father when it came to sports. When I had nine years clean I was watching an NFL game with my father while we were waiting for my mother to finish the Thanksgiving Turkey. As he watched the game, he was hypercritical of the quarterback, receivers, offensive line and the coach. You get the idea. He probably never played football past the age of ten, and he had something to say about everybody. It is just the way he is. If I had that wisdom at the age of seven, I would of saved myself a lot of pain when my father watched my sports games. All he had to do was look at me, and I felt I was being judged and compared to someone else on my team.

I got picked on a lot when I was younger. I actually remember getting picked on, verbally abused, and emotionally abused as an adult until the age of 29. That is the age I entered recovery and found loving people that were not abusive. Kids can be mean and install some serious damage. When our self-esteem is low, we will attract constant abuse. If I was called a name, I believed what others said most of the time. Either way, emotional abuse can be painful.

I went to summer camp from the age of seven until I was fifteen. I went to a different camp than the one that I had the accident from the age of nine until fifteen. When I was nine years old I got picked on for my clothes. My mother rarely sent me to camp with clothes I felt comfortable in. Most of the clothes I was sent to camp with were hand-me- downs from the kids down the street. All your clothes in summer camp had to be labeled with your name for the purpose of sorting laundry. When laundry was sorted, my underwear had three names. It had my name and the names of the two boys from down the street when they went to camp. The other children would tear me up and call me names like scumbag. They would call my family poor. The sad thing was is that I knew my family was not poor. My mother was driving a brand new Jaguar that they payed cash for, but she refused to buy me some clothes that would prevent me from getting picked on. I didn't understand this, but I lived under a belief that I was not worthy of wearing underwear without others peoples names. I judged my self-worth by the way that others accepted me.

All these limiting beliefs lead to low self-worth and low self-esteem. When you don't love yourself it becomes easy to put chemicals in your body and practice in self-destructive behavior. My drug use lasted from the age of eighteen until the age of 29 when I entered recovery. Before I found a solution in recovery, I managed to abstain from using for a few days. I never stayed clean and would start to label myself a failure.

The journey of recovery has allowed me to completely transform my life. I entered recovery as a fearful, lost dishonest victim. I was not good enough, unworthy, and I didn't matter. Some of these things were true and some were limiting beliefs that were real to me. Recovery allows us to transform and discover who we really are. I discovered that I am a powerful, compassionate, authentic, visionary leader. Remember, you are not your past. Once you discover your authentic self, you will experience a freedom like never before. You will then be able to step into your power and start to create your dream life. You will have the ability to recreate your life because you will not be in your own way. By looking at your past you will come to understand that you have a lot to give others. By claiming your freedom, you will clear the path for others to be free. I promise you that the gift is in the giving.

RECREATING OUR LIFE

When I entered recovery, I was given a lot of hope. I was shown that the gift of recovery was a perfect opportunity to completely transform my life. Because I was going to so many meetings, I had the privilege of hearing so many success stories on a regular basis. I heard many stories of people who went from years of homelessness or prison to creating an abundant and meaningful life. I started to see recovery as an opportunity to recreate my life.

Before we recreate our life, we must clean up the wreckage of our past. I came into recovery with an overwhelming amount of financial wreckage. I am grateful that my first sponsor would always bring me back to the present moment by redirecting my focus. If I started projecting or worrying about my overwhelming financial situation he would remind me to focus on staying clean and changing. I was reminded that I had everything I needed in the present moment such as a roof over my head and food in my belly.

I was a financial trader and entered recovery owing my firm $80,000. I also had $50,000 in credit card debt from my drug use. My parents payed-off my credit card debt so I could avoid financial bankruptcy. My parents agreed to put a roof over my head until I payed them back every single penny. My father gave me $20 dollars a week which was just enough to put gas in my car. That was just enough gas to go to meetings and go to the job that did not give me a paycheck. If I wanted to go out to eat with my friends in recovery, someone had to pay my way. This was all very humbling, since I was sometimes making thousands of dollars in a day the year before. I became a financial trader in 1997 and got to experience the tech stock boom until the crash in the year 2000. I was no wolf of wall street, but for a while I was making enough money to afford me a $1000 a day Oxycontin habit. When the stock market crashed, I had nothing to show but the $1000 a day habit. I always joke around and say that God crashed the stock market, so I could get clean. If I would of kept making money, I would have soon died. Within a year of making a lot of money, I was collecting change on the ground. I averaged about $1 a day. This was in recovery. I have no regrets about this huge lesson in humility.

Addiction takes some people from Park Avenue to a park bench. Addiction took me from six figures in the bank and zero debt to my old room in my parents house. I became very grateful for my ugly financial situation. This allowed me to keep my focus on staying clean and changing my insides. I observed many people relapse and die because they fixed their financial situation too quickly. They never gave themselves a chance to build the foundation of recovery. I watched a lot of people get clean and focus on fixing up their outsides. The instant gratification of money and a new car would deprive them of the motivation to work on themselves. They would not see the urgency in living by spiritual principles. I observed that social acceptability does not equal recovery. I observed many people who would get a job working in a phone room making a couple of thousand dollars a week in early recovery. Most phone rooms are not a breeding ground for practicing spiritual principles such as honesty and integrity. I observed many people new to recovery driving a new fancy car and appear that they are living large but they are really dying on the inside. I watched many of these people die from addiction or end up in prison. I am not saying that this is the case for every person who works in a phone room. I am saying that this is a common pattern for people in recovery. If you want to stay clean and transform your life, your decisions and actions must line up with spiritual principles. Everyone in recovery will make mistakes, and principles are a place to stand by, but the decisions we make will shape our destiny.

For my first eleven months clean, I rarely had money in my pocket. I had been going to work every day to a job that was not giving me a paycheck. I was getting tired of not having money in my pocket. I had started to become a better employee. Recovery was teaching me too show up early, stay late, and practice honesty and integrity. Because of my new found honesty and integrity, I was practicing better communication skills. My boss had noticed a significant difference in me and asked what had recently changed in my life. I told him I was in recovery from drug addiction. He said whatever you are doing to keep it up. He said that he sees a completely different version of me and he likes it. He said that he respected the fact that I was committed to paying him back the $80,000 that I owed him for bad trading decisions. Business had been extremely slow because of the tech bubble crash a couple of years before.

Because business was so slow, I asked if I could take a couple of days off to work on a fishing charter boat. Fishing was always a passion of mine. My little brother was a captain and knew of a boat that needed a mate. My boss was fine with it because he knew that I had no money in my pocket. I was excited and grateful to be able to make some money. The first day on the boat went pretty well. We caught some fish and I did a great job talking with the clients. On the second day we caught a big sailfish. The captain told me that we were going to convince the clients to do taxidermy with the fish. Charter boats make 50% commissions on taxidermy.The clients did not want to do taxidermy. The captain told me to do whatever it takes to get the clients to make a deposit with their credit card. The captain was telling me to lie and practice manipulation. This was against the principles that I was committed to practicing in recovery. Recovery has taught me to practice principles with the intention of providing loving service.

I was grateful that I made some money for a couple of days, but I stopped working on that boat because I was not going to compromise the principles that were giving me a new life. The next morning I was back in the office. My boss seemed very happy to see me. He said I hope you are not planning to take any more time off. He said, I have a proposition for you. He said that his plans were to expand the office and bring in new traders. At the same time, he was planning to start another business. He said that I will show you how to manage this office so I can focus on the new business. He said that he would offer me a handsome salary but 75% of the money will go toward the balance of money that I owed the firm. He said that he would even let me start to trade again with a small amount of money. He said that the change he had seen in me gave him enough confidence to make me the manager of the office. This was an incredible opportunity to make all of my financial amends. All I did was practice some spiritual principles such as faith and honesty and opportunity presented itself. I was starting to learn that God works when we step out of the way.

Within three years I paid back the firm, my parents, and every business that I stole from in my addiction. My parents had paid off my $50,000 in credit card debt when I got clean. I also had stolen another $20,000 from my father. My mother kept a ledger of every single penny that I owed them. When I finally paid my mother back the last of what I owed, she started to cry. The look on her face was priceless. In recovery we do not make amends to be forgiven by others, but it can be an added benefit of doing the next right thing. We make amends because it is the right thing to do and we get to forgive ourselves. We no longer have to carry any guilt from our past. Carrying guilt can be like walking around with heavy rocks in all our pockets. Once we have cleared the wreckage of our past, we truly can experience the present moment and start to create our compelling future.

I had cleared up all my financial wreckage. I started to re-establish credit. I had just bought a brand new pick up truck for cash. It was my first recovery vehicle. I was starting to save money. I was starting to travel and experience financial freedom. One day I was in the office and started to stare out the window at a giant Palm tree. The leaves were not moving at all. This showed me that there was no wind outside and that the ocean was very calm. I called my little brother who was out on the ocean with a fishing charter. He said that the ocean was beautiful and that all three of his clients were fighting fish. This made my adrenaline start to pump and I started to feel that I no longer belonged in an office. I decided to pick up a book called "Letting Your Heart Sing." I read the title and the preface and got an excellent idea to quit my job as a financial trader. I know my work in that office was complete because the God of my understanding was starting to talk to me. Our conscious contact with our higher power will sometimes talk to us through dreaming. I believe that are dreams are meant to be followed. I believe dreams are spiritual vision and are not meant to be confused with fantasy.

I started to talk to people in my support group about quitting my job as a financial trader. Nobody told me that I was crazy but the little voice in my own head. That was a voice that was probably planted by my parents. Somebody did ask me "what are you planning to do?" I said "God has big plans for me and I know I am meant for greatness. Until I see the big picture, I am going to follow a childhood dream and become a fisherman. I did know that I never wanted to work a nine to five job ever again. I wanted to be my own boss and make my own hours. My little brother was a fishing guide and a commercial fisherman. Whenever I would go commercial fishing with him he would say "just another day in the office." I always thought that the ocean and bay would make a great office.

I was so close to making this big decision, but I had one fear. I was afraid of what my parents were going to say. I was the broker on my father's account so I felt obligated to stay in that profession. I was also concerned with my parent's approval. After some heavy prayer and meditation I got complete clarity. I came to the realization that my parents tried to completely control my life since I was a young child. Unlike my little brother, I did everything to make my parents happy. It was my parents idea for me to follow in my father's footsteps and trade stocks. I was living someone else's dream. I didn't know I had a choice in the matter. I never had a voice in my own life. Not having a voice lead to no self-esteem and unhappiness. Not having a voice in your own life will also keep you from developing and growing. Not having a voice suppresses creativity and prevents dreaming. I realized that I love myself, and had faith to follow the path that I saw in my dreams. Recovery has taught me that I could have total freedom. It was time for me to take complete control of my own happiness. Because I had made financial amends to my parents, I had no financial attachment to them. I gave myself the freedom to do whatever I wanted, as long as it lined up with spiritual principles.

I became committed to my decision. I told my boss that I would be resigning in one month. I came home and told my parents. My father was understanding and supportive. My mother started to scream and I thought "oh well, that is what my mother does." I know today that she did not want to give up control. If she gave up control, she would have had to look at herself or focus the control on someone else. I realized that the only thing that makes my mother happy is Disney World. I became committed to living my dream life because there is no other way to live.

My experience has shown me that living your dream life is not easy and you are required to constantly get out of your comfort zone. Living your dream life comes with it's challenges. My first challenge was my health.Being a fishing guide could be physically challenging. When I had two years clean I had hurt my back and had a condition called sciatica. I had a herniated disc in my lower back and the pain would radiate down my leg. It would only hurt when I was standing up. I became use to the pain for quite a while because I was in acceptance. As a recovering addict, I did not even consider pain medication. Pain medication is not a solution but a mask of pain. I am committed to always living my life in solutions and not problems. It was easier for me to deal with a whole lot of pain then run risk of relapse. The thought of active addiction made the horrible pain in my leg non-existent.

I was starting to take a couple of fishing charters and was excited about my new line of work. I was living my dream but it came along with a pain in my ass. Sciatica is literally a pain in your ass. Taking fishing charters requires a lot of manual labor. My pain was getting worst each time I took another charter. I went to an acupuncturist and chiropractor for a couple of months with no relief. I than tried to do physical therapy with zero relief. I eventually went to an orthopedic doctor who looked at my MRI and said that I would need a surgery from a neurosurgeon. Immediately, I started to experience financial fear. I asked the doctor "how much is a surgery?" He said "probably about $50,000." For a moment, I felt helpless. I told him that I did not have health insurance. I said that I can't get health insurance with a pre-existing condition. This was when you could not get health insurance with a pre-existing condition. He said lie about it. I knew that lying could be a quick way to end up with a needle in my arm. Recovery and my past experience has taught me that I never have to compromise a spiritual principle. I was feeling stuck. The fear I was experiencing was causing me to rationalize and justify compromising a spiritual principle. I was even starting to second guess the decision to follow my dream. I took my inventory and got quiet. I realized that I should just keep practicing faith and perseverance. Practicing spiritual principles has never failed me before and I believe they never will. I turned this one over to God. I kept taking some charters and pushing through the increasing pain.

One morning I picked up two clients from a fancy hotel. They jumped on the boat and we immediately had great Rappaport. I have no idea why, but I asked them what they did for a living. They responded and said that they were neurosurgeons who specialize in back surgery. Ah ha! The kind universe was showing up. I told them my situation. I then asked how much could I get the surgery that I needed without insurance. They said that if I pay cash, I could probably get the surgery and one night stay in the hospital for under $10,000. That was a big difference then $50,000. I never knew that medical expense could be negotiated with cash. My sponsor that I have had for the past thirteen years has taught me to always get all the facts and not to make decisions based on misinformation. I know today to always find out what is possible.

I was referred to a highly recommended neurosurgeon by several people I knew in recovery. I had to practice patience because it took three more months to get an appointment with his office and two more months to get a surgery date.This doctor was worth the wait. I had several fears about having a surgery. My main fear was financial in nature.   I was hoping those other doctors were right about getting the whole surgery for less than $10,000. I had a fear that the surgery might not be successful. I had a fear that the doctor would tell me that I would have to take pain medication after the surgery. Most doctors do not understand addiction, and will not respect your recovery. I have learned to protect my clean date. I don't let anything get in the way of my recovery. I also had a fear that the recovery time would be long and I would be missing work.

This doctor was sent from God. He had the ability to listen. He was very compassionate to my situation. He happened to have a family member that was in recovery. The doctor assured me that after the surgery I was going to be out of pain immediately. He said there will be no need for pain medication. He said I would be back to work in three weeks. He could not give me the exact details about the cost because he said it was mandatory that I spend a night in the hospital. He did manage to tell me about something called Primary Care which was supplementation through the county.

I had all my ducks in a row and just had to wait for the surgery date. I was still being consumed by financial fear. One day I was sitting in a meeting and someone shared about becoming entirely ready to have God remove the defect of fear.

I felt complete identification. I immediately was willing to turn this whole situation over to God. I had already taken personal responsibility and did my part. My experience is God will move mountains if I bring the shovel and are willing to dig. My financial fears were installed by my parents who always had a scarcity mindset even though they always had money. I realized that through the experience of waiting for my surgery that fear has never served me. Love is always the answer. Just because I become entirely ready to have God remove a defect of character, does not mean that it disappears and never comes back. Fear is a normal human emotion that is the root of all my other defects. I became willing to let it go and practice faith.

Before you know it, I was down stairs in the lobby of the hospital on the morning of my surgery. I was so filled with anxiety, but God sent me an angel in that moment. I ran into a woman named Lorraine that I knew well from recovery. She sat with me until I was taken to pre-operation. I was sitting in pre-operation and hooked up to an IV. All I could do is pray. I felt so much anxiety. I had already settled up with the hospital and surgeon's office. The total bill came to $8800. I was happy about that but I was still filled with fear. I kept turning the whole situation over. I knew that the medical staff and surgeon were a power greater than me and that God was going to work through them. All of the sudden one of the nurses gets told that they cannot do my surgery. There was someone who needed an emergency brain surgery. I was told that my surgery will be 10 days later. My initial thought was self-centered in nature and made me upset, but I understood. I became more concerned about the life of the person who needed the emergency surgery.

I realized that I had really turned this situation over.

I finally had the surgery. I woke up in post-operation to my girlfriend and sponsor. All sorts of people that I knew from recovery showed up to visit. My pain was gone. A few days later, I had a post-operation appointment. The first thing the doctor asked was "How many meetings have you been to since the surgery?" That is my kind of doctor. He knew that my recovery was the most important thing in my life.

Within a few weeks, I was back on the water and living my dream. I was pain free. After the whole experience, I was so grateful for all of the lessons that came through the experience. Most of all, I learned that the universe will always show up for me when I am committed to doing the next right thing.

Within a couple of years I built up a pretty good business when the country was in a recession. The economy was terrible, but my phone was ringing. The secret to my success was applying the spiritual principle of service. One of the only things that I learned in college was that it takes more money to get a new customer than keep an existing one. Existing clients keep coming back when you provide an abundance of service. I never advertised. My clients did my marketing. I was spending 200 days of the year on the water. I was truly living a childhood dream. Witnessing incredible sunrises was part of my daily routine. Mother nature would bless me with challenges all the time. Every day was a new experience and was an opportunity to learn something new.

After 10 years of making a living on the water, I was starting to notice a lot of environmental issues. I started to be proactive and make phone calls to various agencies in the state of Florida. I got nowhere. I felt like I was being ignored or nobody cared. Finally, I got on the phone with someone from a nonprofit that gave me a lot of information. She had a concern for the environment. I started to cry on the phone with her because I was suffering from a broken heart. I finally realized that I was not alone. There were others that cared, but the fight was with the politicians of the state of Florida and the lobbyists that support them.

Watching the environment get destroyed was not only breaking my heart but it was causing me to become cynical. Fear was creeping in and I would start to experience depression. I was starting to feel victimized. One of my first lessons in recovery was that victims stay stuck. I was definitely stuck and I chose empowerment over victimization. Human beings are given the power of decision. I get to choose what things mean and what to focus on. Once I had some clarity, I realized that the universe was starting to talk to me. Just like God gave me an invitation to not work in an office trading stocks, the universe was showing me that it was time to move on. The universe was showing me that the time has come to start living your true purpose.

When I left my office job, the plan was to become a fisherman until I figured out the bigger picture. The problem is that I ended up getting stuck in my comfort zone. The bigger picture is me living my purpose. The bigger picture is me making a monumental impact on this world. My true passion is recovery and transformation. I have known for several years that I am meant to be a motivational speaker. I love to empower others because I see the greatness in people. I see this because someone looked at me when I was at the lowest point in my life and what they saw was infinite possibility.

"Look at a man the way he is and he only becomes worse, but look at him as if he were what he could be, then he becomes what he should be."

Johann Wolfgang Von Goethe

I knew it was time to start to pursue my dream life. I had to get the hell out of my comfort zone. Your comfort zone could kill you. My comfort zone was leading me toward depression.

"The comfort zone is the graveyard for all potential and hope. It is where dreams go to die. It is where lack, mediocrity, and low expectations thrive."

Berta Medina Garcia

My past experience has shown me that nothing great ever happened in my comfort zone. Through observation of my own transformation in recovery I became visionary. If I can transform my life in recovery, than so can anyone who is willing to surrender to a completely new way of life. I am talking about a life of total freedom and infinite possibility. My vision is that everyone gets to heal, transform, and awaken. Recovery is the opportunity to completely transform your life. I have learned that the only thing that will get in the way of my dreams is me. If you don't have dreams than discover who you are. When you discover your authentic self you will be free from your past suffering and begin to dream. Recovery has allowed me to become the master of my own destiny.

Get busy living or get busy dying.

Steven Spielberg